Rosemary Ridley at age

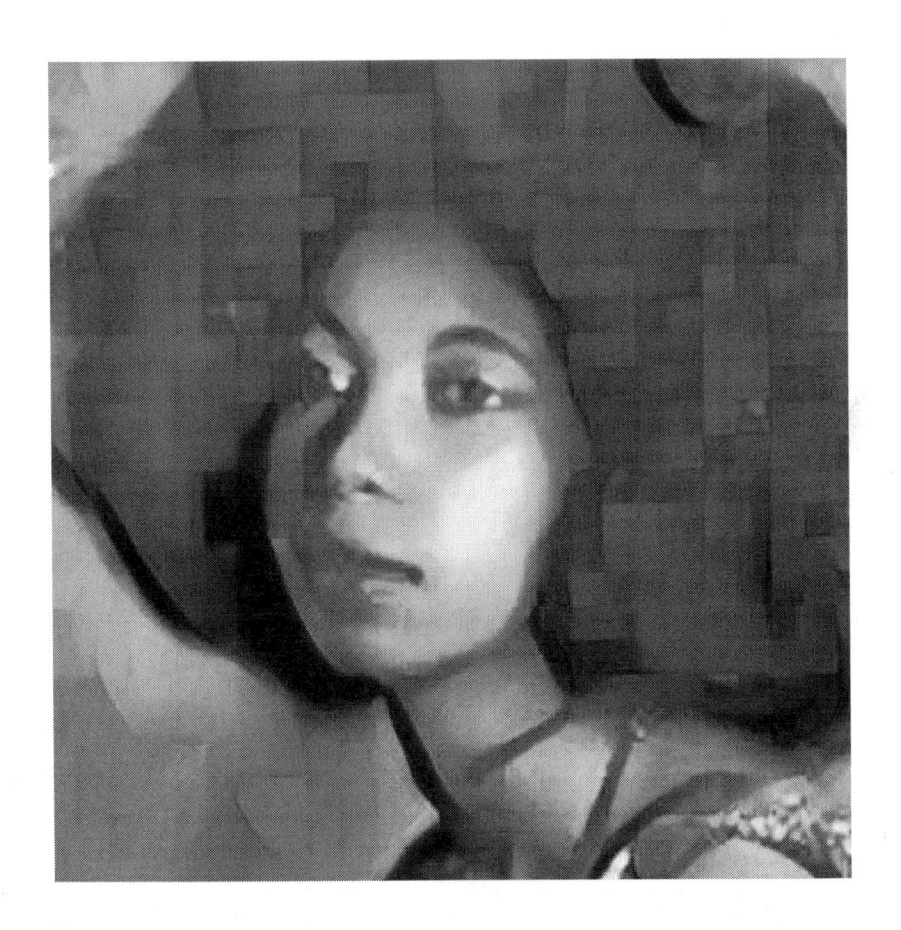

Rosemary Ridley Vines is CEO/founder at Reconstructed Women's Fellowship Ministry, Inc. **It** was first established in 2001. The ministry's main goal is to help rebuild, restore, and empower those who have been subjected to the horrendous effects of domestic and sexual violence. Rosemary is an advocate against domestic, sexual, and family violence and her goal is to help raise awareness toward a global disease that torments many homes. For speaking engagements, seminars, or conferences, please send her an email at rosemary.vines@yahoo.com. I want to give a special thank you to my husband Charles Vines, and to my sister Maria McKinsey, who encouraged me to write my book. To my five children (Donnie, Alesia, Tristaca, Joy, and Willie), to my thirteen grand-children, and a special thank you to all of my readers! Love you so much!

*\*\*:My book is in no way written to destroy anyone's name or reputation. What have been recorded are true incidents that took place in my life. Some names and specific details have been changed to protect the privacy of individuals. It is only written to walk you through my life and to share the healing power of Jesus Christ. \*\**

Rosemary Ridley Vines   (Author)

"Beauty for Ashes" The Life Story of Rosemary

Well, where can I begin? First of all, I am thankful to my Lord and Savior Jesus Christ for giving me the ability to share my story. He is and always will be my best friend. I have put off writing my book for such a long time because I just couldn't seem to find the time to sit down and begin the process. I also believe that I dreaded going back into my past because of so much pain that I experienced. Through God's grace, I will allow you into my life as I unfold my life story of how God gave me beauty for ashes, the oil of joy for mourning, the garment of praise for the spirit of heaviness (Isaiah 61:3). My life has been one that has been filled with abuse, pain, loss, and sorrow. Throughout my book, I will take you on a journey with me as I reveal to you my weaknesses and my strengths, my triumphs and my failures, my laughter and my tears. "Beauty for Ashes" is especially dedicated to my mom, Mrs. Mary Ida Evans Ridley (affectionately known as "Mom'mie), who managed to take care of her children the best she could in spite of the horrendous abuse she endured. Now I want you to relax in your favorite chair and turn the pages of my book as I invite you into the life story of Rosemary.

# Chapter 1

Growing up in an unhealthy environment with an alcoholic and abusive father caused a great deal of pain in my life. I was the youngest of six siblings, which were two boys and four girls. I have heard people say that you shouldn't have a favorite family member, but I must confess that my sister Lorraine was my favorite. She was the one that I could run to when I felt that I was being bullied. She was the one that would pick up a brick and throw it at you if you bothered her baby sister. She was my hero. She was my friend.

I will take you back now when we were very small children. Not knowing what to expect on a daily basis, we found ourselves being frightened, hurt, angry, and confused. I could never understand how my mother could allow us to be subjected to so much violence and abuse. I always thought that I had a very pretty mother, but somewhere in her life, something happened to her to cause her to have such a low self-esteem. Whenever you see a person allowing another individual to have complete control over their life, there has to be a deeper problem that the victim has suppressed within their subconscious. Domestic violence is a horrible disease that affects all that is involved and can leave lasting effects if not dealt with properly. It is amazing after so many years that I can still remember the difficult times that we endured in that little house in Farmville, N.C. So many unanswered questions even to this day. Why didn't my mom ever leave him? So tired of the same thoughts that continued to whirl around in my mind, yet I never received an answer. How can you love someone that abused your children right before your eyes? We were supposed to be protected, love and nurtured. Instead, we were beat with belts, threatened with knives, and isolated from our best friends. In elementary school, I can remember so well walking to and from school holding tight to my books with my head hung down. For some unknown reason, I felt a sense of security and protection as I held my books tight to my chest. I was so afraid that someone would pick at me. I never walked in a straight line. I would always walk from one side of that dirt road to the other side until I reached home. If I didn't see Lorraine when the school bell rang, I would feel absolutely terrified. She wasn't as timid as I was and wasn't afraid to stand up to anybody just to protect me. Going through elementary school was very challenging. As I before stated, it was six of us and we didn't have as much as some of the other students had. I remember vividly the old pump that was on the side of the house where we lived in Farmville, It is amazing that I can still remember the address: 103 Humphrey Street. I guess it is because so much abuse took place there for years. When you have traumatic experiences, they are often suppressed in our subconscious as the memory lies dormant within us. We are not aware that so much pain can be hidden within us until something unpleasant happens and all the pain and anger rises to the surface and is exposed. Unfortunately, many times the exposure of pain is not a pretty sight to behold. Anyway, back to the house on 103 Humphrey Street. I remember the large cement porch, iron rails that my sisters and I used to climb on to get on top of the house (lol), and the wooden swing that hung from the ceiling of the front porch. Those were fun times when my sister Lorraine and I would swing back and forth as high as we could go. Maybe that old swing was a way of helping us to cope with what we were going through in our young life. My dad was a barber and I remember him making my mom wash his white shirts, hang them dry, starch and then press each shirt every day. He was a very neat and well-dressed man and if my mom didn't iron his shirts just right or didn't have his barber towels ready for him, she would get hit in her face with his fist. How it broke my heart to see blood run down my mother's face! I hated my dad! I wished many times that he would die and disappear from off the face of the earth! I just wanted to see my mother happy. Why was she choosing this type of life? She was such a beautiful lady with coal black hair that hanged down her back. She could have gotten anyone that she wanted, but she chose to stay with this abusive man that always treated her like she was a slave. It has been many years now but I can feel the sadness in my soul as I write this book and share what my mom endured. Each time she sat on the front porch she could not sit facing the traffic. My dad always made her turn her chair around and face the huge picture window or the front door. Me being the youngest girl, I just could not fathom in my mind why my dad made my mom do such things. The only thing I knew was it was hurting me to see her treated this way. She was such a loving person and had such a gentle spirit. It is sad to think that she believed that this was the kind of love she deserved. There was one time when she asked where he had been and he hit her across the head with a broken chair leg, splitting her scalp wide open. With blood-drenched hair, she took care of her own wound instead of him taking her to a doctor. If only I had the courage to fight him back! Why did he stay there with her? Why didn't he just leave? Surely he couldn't have loved her.

I remember my two brothers who were much older, or so I thought, and the sadness I felt when my dad put them out. James was 17 years old and Percell was 16. Why was he doing this? I just couldn't understand what provoked my dad to such behavior. I didn't want my big brothers to leave us. I still can recall my mom pleading with him not to send the boys away at such an early age. I can remember the sound of her voice as she wept in her bedroom; a sound I will never forget of a heart-broken mother. Yet, she still chose to remain with this man whom I saw as a beast. Ignoring my mom's pleas, he sent them off to Newark, New Jersey driving a black 1950's Oldsmobile car. Where were they going? Where would they live? How would they make it with a few dollars in their pocket? Unfortunately, I never found out the whole story behind how my brothers survived. I never heard anyone talking about how they made it. I did find out later on that Percell eventually became a barber in New Jersey but I never found out how my brother James survived. Sadly enough, they found James in his bed deceased from a massive heart-attack at the age of 32. I was told that he drank strong alcohol and had become addicted to it. Of course I blamed my dad for this. Ironically enough, at the age of 58, they found my brother Percell deceased in his bed from a heart-attack that was caused by a severe asthma attack. Was all of this pain my two brother's fault? How could such misfortune happen to the both of them, yet they died early deaths? I guess I will always have questions that will never be answered in this life-time.

Well, we four girls began to mature and grow into beautiful young ladies. We were known as the "pretty Ridley girls" from Farmville. But because of the abuse that we all endured from our father, we all had self-esteem issues. Some of the girls at school were jealous of us because we were light-skinned. I never understood why people with lighter complexions were always stereotyped. Little did they know of the inward and outward wars we faced because of the way we were being treated at home. I could never figure out why the girls were jealous of us when most of our clothes were "hand-me-downs" or came from the second hand store. Today these stores are known as thrift shops or consignment shops but back in the 60's they were known as second hand stores. Why? Because someone else had worn them before you did. There was also this sweet older lady that was a friend to my mom. She would always bring us bags of clothes and coats to wear to school in the winter months. I really loved Mrs. Artis but I would dread going through that bag of clothes each time she brought them over to the house. I remember one time my sister Myrtle, who was next to my oldest sister Maria, wore a big old white fur coat to school. So many of her classmates picked at her and laughed at that coat. I don't think she never wore that coat again. Each year it was the same old thing. We were always wearing used clothes or either wearing each other's clothes. I will never forget that big tin tub that sat in our kitchen. Our mother would fill it with warm water and all four girls would take a bath in the same water. There was a clothes line that she hung across the kitchen from one end of the wall to the other end. She would wash our under garments out every night with her wash tub and wash board and hang them to dry on that home-made clothes line. I remember going to school hungry some mornings. There were also times that we didn't have any money to buy our lunch tokens. Thankfully, I had a close friend that I would like to mention in my book. Her name is Ella Barnes. She would always share her bologna sandwich with me. I thought that was the best sandwich I had ever eaten before! Sometimes she would share her peanut butter crackers with me. I never forgot what Ella did for me. She was my true friend.

The summer months were a lot better for us because my mom had a large garden in the back yard of our house on Humphrey Street. Before I continue to talk about the garden, I have to mention the times that Lorraine and I would walk the railroad track that led into the woods. We would always carry brown paper bags to fill them with the red juicy plums that grew on the trees. I wonder whatever happened to those plum trees. Anyway, back to the garden. I believe that they grew everything possible in that garden. Lorraine and I also used to enjoy digging the white potatoes from under the ground, picking the cucumbers and the squash, and helping our mom shuck the corn. I have to mention the large, red tomatoes that we picked right off the vine and ate them with salt. I can still see my mom (who we called ("Mom'mie) in my mind chopping, sweating and wiping her face with that old apron that she wore every day. She worked diligently in that hot sun making sure we had enough food to eat each day. With **all** of her hard work and loyalty to my dad, it seemed as though he was never satisfied. We cringed each time we heard him come home at night. What would happen next?

## Chapter 2

We never had a doubt in our mind when our dad would walk through that door in a drunken state because he would always give us a sign with that eerie whistling noise that he made with his mouth… a loud whistle followed by a low, deep whistle. Oh, how I hated that sound! I knew each time what was about to take place. My poor mom would meet him at the door dreading what would take place next. Why did she have to accept being treated this way? How could she love a man that didn't love her back? Couldn't you see your four girls sitting close together on the couch afraid to even m o v e one inch? My mother had a very gentle, soft-spoken voice and she tried many times to calm my dad with her words but it never seemed to work. She would always say, "Honey, can't you please just sit down and rest and not bother the girls?" Of course her words didn't mean a thing. I always believed that he was just an angry man that wanted to take out his frustrations on his wife and children. He would ignore my mom's cries and make us stand in a straight line and whip us for no reason at all. A few times Mom'mie would try to intervene just to get a sharp blow to her head, eye, or mouth. It really didn't matter where he hit her. I hated seeing blood run from my mom's face or her lip. I was such a frail, skinny little girl. I wished in my soul that I was big enough to beat him up. Here we are standing in a line being beat for nothing. I was brought up saying my prayers every night but was God actually real? Where were you God when my mom was being beaten senseless? Where was He when my dad kicked her so hard in her private area that she had to go to the doctor to get stitches in order to stop the bleeding? Where was God when my mom shielded her head with her hands and four of her fingers were broken? I was only a child and I couldn't understand why all of these bad things continued to happen to us. Why couldn't we have a normal, happy family like I saw on the television stories? Little did I know that these television sitcoms were fictitious and not a reality. The National Coalition Against Domestic Violence (N.C.A.D.V.) defines it as the willful intimidation, physical assault, battery, sexual assault, and/or other abusive behavior perpetrated by an intimate partner against another. It is an epidemic affecting individuals in every community, regardless of age, economic status, race, religion, nationality, or educational background. Violence against women is often accompanied by emotionally abusive and controlling behavior, and thus is part of a systematic pattern of dominance and control. Domestic violence results in physical injury, psychological trauma, and sometimes death. Please read this last statement carefully: "**The consequences of domestic violence can cross generations and truly last a lifetime**" (National Sexual Violence Resource Center). I needed to digress from my story to include information that is pertinent to the reader that may be found in similar situations. The information provided is to help bring awareness toward domestic violence. The final decision is left entirely up to the individual. Now let me continue with my story. Not only were we victims of domestic abuse, but we were also not allowed to have dark skinned friends. I'm sure you know what my next statement is going to be. You guessed it! Most of our friends were dark-skinned. How could our dad tell us that he/she was too dark to be our friend? Thankfully, our friends knew that we were not stuck up or arrogant because of our light skin tone. Each time one of our friends would come over after school, they would run out the back door when we saw our dad driving up. There was a time that my dad came home early from work and saw my sister Lorraine and her best friend Annie walking from school. I was walking right behind them and when I saw the look on my dad's face, fear began to race all over my body. I could actually feel my heart palpitating underneath my blouse. I remember Annie's face also had a look of fear and anger. I hated going into that house! Praying silently I began to ask God to please protect my sister. Annie lived on the street behind us, so she hurried home and didn't walk Lorraine to our house, as she normally did. No sooner than Lorraine walked into the house, my dad punched her in her right eye. Because of her complexion, it didn't take long for the swelling and dark bruise to come underneath her eye. Immediately after punching her, he took out his hawk-billed knife and held it to her throat and dared her to talk to another dark-skinned person. I remember calling his name out really loud as I begged him not to hurt Lorraine. I tried to pull his arm and the knife away from my sister's throat, but he turned and threatened to hit me also. With a snarling voice he shouted to me to get out of his way. How I hated my dad! Why didn't he just leave? If I only had the nerve to fight him back! If he hated my mom and us so much, why didn't he just go away?! I can't count the times that I asked God to make him die. I found out later on in my life that my dad resented his biological father for things that happened when he was young that I never got a clear understanding of. All I know is that he was taking all of his anger out on us and our dear mom. I could always see the pain in my mom's eyes each time our dad would abuse us. She tried so hard to protect us, but it always ended up with her being beaten also. My sister and I both stood in the hallway of our home frightened and in tears. Afraid to move, our mother encouraged us to go into the other room. As soon as she attempted to get us to a more safe area, my dad immediately hit her and shoved her into the bedroom closet. There were times he would make my mom sit in a dark closet for hours on a card board box. I remember hearing her faint sobs throughout the house. Words cannot express how it made me feel to hear my mom cry inside that dark closet. In my heart, I could not understand why she remained in such a horrible situation. I loved my mom very much, but many times I held anger towards her because of what she allowed her children to endure. She knew that her life was threatened so many times, but what was the underlying cause that made her remain in such an abusive relationship? She was a very beautiful lady, but did she have very little self-worth? There were times when I saw my mom cutting her arm in a violent rage with a knife. Lord please have mercy on my mother! A person that remains in an unhealthy environment obviously has an embedded root cause. If we never seek counsel and help, we will always see ourselves with little value. Ultimately, we will end up in abusive relationships and accept this kind of treatment as true love. Unfortunately, the same cycle happened to my sisters and me.

My mother was always a quiet person and shared very little with her children. As I think back today, I often find myself wishing she had spent more quality time with us. Maybe I would have understood her better and why she chose to live a life that offered little hope. Unfortunately, most of her time was spent taking care of my dad and helping him to recover from his weekend alcohol binges. There were so many tell-tale signs of abuse that I am so familiar with today that took place in our home. However, as a child, I had no clue of recognizing these signs. I only knew that I wished my mom would leave and take her children out of such an unhealthy environment. Instead of seeking help, she was always trying to think of ways to satisfy my dad, although her ideas hardly ever worked. Our grand-mother, who we called "Big Ma," lived in a small town known as Scotland Neck, N.C. My dad hardly ever allowed us to go and visit her, which left a very faint memory of her in my mind. I can only remember her having long, silky black hair that hang down her back and beautiful legs that caught my attention as she sat on her front porch. Strangely enough, the only words that stayed with me that she spoke was when she asked for Myrtle, which was my older sister, because she favored "Big Ma" a great deal. That is the only time that I can remember my dad taking us to visit our grand-mom. I was only around eleven years old during the time and was heart-broken because I couldn't spend more time with her. The next time we visited Scotland Neck was to attend my grand-mom's funeral. My dad had been drinking that day which caused us to arrive at the funeral very late. I remember the rain coming down very hard that day. As we were pulling up to the church, my mom jumped out of the car and ran into the church hoping to see her mother one more time. As she approached the door of the church, the coffin had already been closed and pushed into the vestibule. Thankfully, the mortician allowed my mom to see her mother one last time. My sisters and I never got the chance to see our grand-mom again. To my readers, I never knew that writing my book would cause me to feel such pain. It has been many years since this has happened, but to bring to surface all that occurred in my life is opening up a hurt that I did not know was still there. Sadly enough, we never had the chance to meet our grand-dad as well. I was told that he was one of the most handsome men in Scotland Neck. I learned later on in life that he passed away in Norfolk, Virginia when I was only in the seventh grade. How could my dad take away such precious moments and memories from our lives? I missed not knowing my grand-mom; I missed not getting the chance to meet my grand-dad! It still hurts, but I know God can take away the pain. Family sources later informed me that my grand-dad (Mr. Balom Evans) is pictured in a photograph with a group of other black men at the Smithsonian Institute in Washington, D.C. He was one of the first black railroad conductors in the 1800's. I am so proud of my grand-dad, although I never had the chance to meet him. I hurt, but God will remove the pain. During my childhood, I knew very little about him. My mom hardly ever mentioned his name. So many unanswered questions! On the other hand, my dad made it his business for us to meet his dad who lived in Goldsboro, N.C. He was the pastor of St. Stephen church in Farmville, N.C. I remember his name as being Reverend Hudson. For some reason our dad used his mom's last name instead of his father's name. That's another mystery I will probably never know the answer to. I remember the times my sister Lorraine and I would spend weekends in Goldsboro with grand-daddy and his wife. I think I was in the sixth grade and Lorraine was in the eighth. My mom passed away in 1993, leaving me with so many unanswered questions and empty places in my life. Why did you stay Mom'mie? Why didn't you come to us and talk to us more? Remember at the beginning of my book that I shared how my dad made my two brothers leave home at an early age? I saw them as my big brothers but that was taken away from me also. There was a time that my brother James came home to visit, but his visit only turned into a violent fight with my dad. After a few attempts to come back home, he finally gave up and we never saw him alive again. The next time I saw him I was fourteen years old. There he laid in a coffin in New Haven, Connecticut. My mom, sisters and I rode the train to James' funeral, but my dad did not go with us. Needless to say, my mom's heart was shattered into a million pieces. How true it is that traumatic experiences remain in your subconscious! I cannot remember the entire funeral, but what I do remember is the deep, heavy sobs that my mom made as she collapsed on her son's lifeless body. Who could ever forget the sound of a mother's cry?

## Chapter 3

My sisters and I began to grow up into beautiful teenagers. I was the youngest so I couldn't date yet, but I remember the young men that my sisters dated. Of course back in those days, the boys could only stay until 10:00 p.m. It used to be so funny to me when one of my sisters had company over. Every Wednesday night (date night) at 10:00 sharp, my mom would walk in the hallway and clear her throat. "Ahem, ahem; it's 10:00," my mom would say loudly. So funny! I would peep in the living room and see the young man jump up and hurry to the front door. However, as we grew older, I started to notice that the guys my sisters were connected to were showing familiar traits that my dad displayed. Little did I know that this was a generational curse that had been passed down from our parents. Each one of my sisters had graduated from high school and had married men that were abusive to them. It is important to note that most of the time when a child or children grow up in domestic violence they believe that threats and violence are the norm in a relationship. They are expected to keep the family secret, sometimes not even talking to each other about the abuse. Is that why I became a "silent sufferer" later on in my life? Is that why I was so afraid to speak up; so afraid to cry out for help? Is that why I took the blame for every bad thing that happened? But I don't want to get ahead of myself as I share with my readers.

Most experts believe that children who are raised in abusive homes learn violence is an effective way to resolve conflicts and problems. Because my mom's attention was mostly on my dad as she constantly tried to keep him from going into one of his violent rages, it left her four girls feeling empty and needy. The end results were my sisters being involved in unhealthy relationships. I was the baby girl and all I could remember was seeing my sisters trying to make a marriage work that was inevitably destined for a break-up.

Being exposed to so much battery, violence and confusion ultimately took its toll on me. After seeing my mom and sisters endure abuse, you would think I would have been more careful in my choice of men. However, I also believed that threats and violence were the norm in a relationship. At the age of sixteen years old, I became pregnant with my first child. Sadly enough, the young man that had impregnated me was very violent and abusive toward me. I don't think there was not a bad name that he didn't call me. I was a junior in high school and was able to keep my grades up on an A & B level. My dad was enraged when he found out that I was carrying a child. Remember, "Traumatic experiences have a tendency of staying with you." I remember my dad calling me into the living room and asking me why I get pregnant by that boy. Immediately after his question, he put a mean look on his face and held a long, brown shot gun on the right side of my temple. Needless to say, I could have easily lost my unborn child because of the fear that had wracked my body. I stood frozen and could not say a word. He demanded that the young man whom I will call "Tim" (not his real name), take me down to the Justice of the Peace and marry me. I remember vividly the words that he snarled at me: "I will not allow a bastard child to come into my house!" Didn't he care that "Tim" was already beating me, stomping me, giving me black eyes and dragging me around?

After being forced into marrying "Tim," the abuse only escalated. At the time, I was still in high school so we were allowed to live with my mom and dad. My dad was a barber and "Tim" only abused me when my dad was at work. It was mostly on the weekends because "Tim" stayed gone most of the time during the week. I was thankful for that. I would like to mention Mr. Leroy Redden, who was the assistant principle at H.B. Sugg School in Farmville, N.C. before I continue on with my story. During the time that I was pregnant, I had gone to school as long as I could until it became too difficult to walk to and from school each day. As I before stated, I was a junior in high school, and it was drawing closer to the end of the school year and was time to take EOG test. I had stopped attending school by now and Mr. Redden noticed that I had not attended in a few weeks. He came out to my house and said, "Ridley, (he always called me by my last name), you are too smart not to be able to go on to your senior year in high school. What I will do is bring your test to your home and allow you to take them here." I was so thankful in my heart and am forever grateful for having a principle like Mr. Redden. He has long since passed away, but I will never forget him. Because of Mr. Redden and the confidence that he had in me, I was able to graduate with my senior class at Farmville Central High School in 1972! By this time, I had a bouncing little baby boy. Now back to my story.

I remember during my senior year at Farmville Central, I had asked "Tim" one Saturday night where was he going as he walked out the front door. He ignored me so I reached for his shoulder to get his attention. As soon as I did that, he immediately turned around and knocked me unconscious in the front yard. When I came back to consciousness, blood was all over my face and blouse. He just left me laying right there in the front yard. I crawled through the grass and unto the front porch and called out to my mom. I could already tell that my lip had been split from the inside out and two of my teeth had been chipped off. When my mom saw me, she just let out a scream and ran into her bedroom and locked the door. I could not get upset with my mom because I knew that her nerves had been frayed because of what my dad was taking her through. She eventually came out of her room and applied ice to my lip that was wrapped up in a white handkerchief. All I remember her repeating under her breath was, "I told "Honey" (the name she called my dad) not to make you marry that boy!" What kind of "Honey" was he to make his baby girl marry such an abusive person? Just because I made a mistake did I deserve this kind of treatment? My mother was very disappointed in my dad making me marry an abuser, but she allowed my dad to treat her the same way. I was a sight for sore eyes when I looked in the bathroom mirror. My lip had swollen out really big and there was a gaping split underneath my top lip. Although my mom held an ice pack to my lip, it only took the swelling down a little. I did not like missing school, so I decided to get dressed the next morning and head to school. I kept a white handkerchief over my mouth all day to hide the swelling. I was so tired of answering questions all that day. I can't count the times that I heard, "Rosemary, what happened?" Of course I told a lie and said that I fell down and hit my mouth on a brick. I will never forget as we were exchanging classes that one of my classmates whose name was Erma Jean, walked up to me and snatched my hand down displaying my ugly, busted and swollen lip. She was being a jokester, but she never knew how much shame and hurt she caused me that day. (Rip Erma Jean). I made it through my senior year, although many times I had to wear a smile to hold back the tears. "Tim" would cheat and lust at other women right in front of my face and dared me to say anything. He gave me the name "redbone" because of my light complexion. I still hate hearing that name today. At the end of my senior year, he moved out and went back to his home town. Free at last, or so I thought.

There was this guy in my senior class that I had fallen deeply in love with, but he was not aware of the deep feelings that I carried in my heart for him. All he knew was that I liked him. I will not mention his name because of what I am about to share. We eventually started dating and I enjoyed riding out with him in his car. It has been so long ago and I cannot remember what make and model car he drove. Anyway, one particular night, he drove down a dirt road and parked. He asked me to get into the back seat with him. Because of my love for him, I complied to his wishes. In the back seat of the car's floor lay a long, wooden stick that looked like it could have come from a tree. The man that I loved made this cold, sordid statement that I did not expect to hear from him: "If you don't have sex with me, I am going to beat you with this stick," he said. After everything was over with, he stated that he enjoyed being with me, but he wasn't going to talk to me anymore. I could not believe what I was hearing. Why are these bad things continuing to happen to me? He showed no signs of abusive behavior prior to this incident. That is why it is so important to get to know your partner before you build trust with them. Because of my home environment and being raised around fear and anxiety, I was too afraid to tell him no. I was left with feelings of being violated alld betrayed. After he dropped me back off to my house, I went to bed and cried myself to sleep. I carried deep hurt for years because of what he did to me and because of the feelings that I had for him. I never told anyone what happened to me on that summer night. After many years and not knowing whatever happened to him, I stumbled across his name one day as I was perusing photos on Classmate.com. There he was just as handsome as he was in high school. I immediately began to pray and ask God to give me the courage to confront him and tell him how bad he had hurt me years ago. I sent him my phone number and he did not hesitate to call me. After I brought up the painful memories of that summer night, he responded in total shock and stated that he had no memory in his mind of anything ever happening like that. I reassured him over and over that it did happen. The trauma happened to me and that is why it was so vivid in my memory. I was thankful that he showed great remorse and stated that he would drive down to my hometown just to give me a personal apology. That was very kind and gallant of him seeing that he lived three to four hours away. I was really happy to see him after so many years. I had already forgiven him, but it made me feel so much better to look in his eyes and to hear him say, "I am so sorry Rosemary." We are still friends today and stay in contact with one another just to say hello.

## Chapter 4

Because "Tim" had moved back to his home town, I was thinking that I was finally free of all of the abuse and beatings. How wrong was I! After graduating from Farmville Central High School, Lorraine and I were hired at a factory in Farmville called U.S.I. Sewing Factory. Boy, was those the days! I enjoyed going to work (sometimes) lol! I enjoyed working beside my friend whose name was Angeline Baptist (Rip). We would race each other on our serge machine each day trying to make commission. I always had a comical streak in me and some days I would get us in trouble because of my shenanigans. Lorraine was eventually promoted to floor supervisor and she showed no mercy toward me. As a matter of fact, I believe she was even harder on me because I was her sister. Those were the days... I eventually started dating another handsome young man and we seemed to be hitting it off pretty good. But here comes the drama again. One night after my friend and I came from the movie theater, we were sitting outside in front of my mom and dad's house. It was a hot summer night so he had his car windows rolled down. For some reason, I can remember the kind of car he drove. It was a green Laguna Super Sport. I don't believe those type of cars exist anymore, but back in the 70's they were nice cars. Anyway, as we sat and talked, a car pulled up abruptly behind us and "Tim" jumped out of the passenger's seat, ran up to my car window, reached inside and knocked me out cold again. Please help my life Lord! During this time, I was only 19 years old. When I came back to consciousness, my friend had got out of the car and was beating him senseless. Remember I told you earlier that Lorraine wasn't afraid to fight anybody when it came to her baby sister? When she heard all of the commotion, she ran outside and jumped right on top of "Tim." She wasn't even concerned about one of those flying fists striking her in the face. She was still kicking and hitting him. It didn't matter that she was short in stature. She was punching and kicking just as hard as she could. There I stood still dazed from the blow that I had sustained on the side of my head. All of a sudden, my dad rushed out of the front door with the same long, brown shot gun that he had held against my head. He told my friend and my sister to get out of the way. Once they ran out of the way, my dad starting shooting. I'm telling you it was pandemonium and chaos on that night! I've never seen a man run as fast as "Tim" did! One of the bullets nearly got him as he was jumping into the getaway car. After that night, I didn't hear anything else from "Tim" for a long time.

Unfortunately, as time passed, a friend of the family made a statement to me that put fear in my heart. I wasn't a Christian at the time and did not understand the Bible at all. It was said to me that once I became married, I could not marry again and if I didn't reunite with my husband, I was going to bum in hell one day. In spite of the horrendous abuse and infidelity that I experienced with "Tim," I contacted him and I and my son moved back into an apartment with him in Wilson, N.C. This was the beginning of greater sorrow and torment. Living in Wilson with "Tim" was pure hell. I thought to myself, "If hell is worse than this, I certainly do not want to go there!" I soon became pregnant with my second child. He was never home on the weekends and we had nothing to eat. Even though I was not saved at the time, God always watched over me. I had met this sweet lady whose name was Mrs. Maye. She knew what I was going through because she could hear him cursing at me and knocking me around, even when I was pregnant with my daughter. We lived above Mrs. Maye and every weekend she would stand outside her front door and yell upstairs for me and my son to come and eat dinner with her. God had her there just for me and my son. And boy could she cook! I will never forget those big, juicy homemade biscuits with a pot of butter beans with fat back meat in the pot! I was so thankful for Mrs. Maye.

The entire nine months of my pregnancy was filled with beatings and horrible words that were spat at me on a weekly basis. I could not understand why God would want me to return to such horror in order to make it into heaven. One particular day as I stood in the bathroom to comb my hair, "Tim" suddenly opened the door and knocked me over into the bath tub. I was seven months pregnant with his daughter and could not believe he knocked me in the bath tub for no reason at all. After falling hard into the tub, he then took his foot and stomped me directly in my stomach. It was only by the grace of the Almighty God that my baby girl was born healthy. There were times that I would run away from him and go downstairs to Mrs. Maye's house until he left for work. I became so tired of him knocking me around for no reason. Whenever he felt like it he would punch me or shove me and then call me illicit names. I was so tired and weary of the beatings.

Nobody had a clue what I was enduring in Wilson. I endured marital rape, dealt with his adulterous affairs, a sexually transmitted disease on two different occasions, loneliness, fear, anxiety, worry, loss of weight (mind you I was already small in size), sadness, bruises, beatings, and name calling. There were times when he would turn me upside down by both of my feet and bang my head on the floor repeatedly. I remember when I was running from him one day and was trying to get out of the front door. I had gotten most of my body out but my left arm was partly inside. When he saw that my arm was still partly inside the door, he slammed the door on my arm as hard as he could. The pain was so intense that it caused me to collapse. Because of the enormous swelling to my arm and fingers, I had to go to the doctor. I had to wear a sling on my arm until the swelling went down. I remember going to Farmville to see my mom and when she saw my arm in a sling, she ran from the front door and ran into her bedroom and started to cry. Again I understood that my mom's nerves were bad. I just couldn't take it anymore! Surely the family friend did not know what he was talking about! As I neared the end of my pregnancy, I began to plan in my mind an escape strategy. I would look for a job, save up my money and get the heck out of hell city! Everything was finally working in my favor. Because of my past experience working in a sewing factory,

I was hired at another sewing factory in Wilson called Carolina Casuals. Mrs. Maye kept my boy and girl each day while I worked. I really miss Mrs. Maye. I felt a freedom of being able to go to work without having to be slapped around. I met wonderful friends at Carolina Casuals and I enjoyed going to work. There was one particular friend that grew very close to me. Her name was Earlene Heath. I often think of her today and wonder where she is. Anyway, Earlene didn't play and was not afraid of anybody. She was a very sweet person, but you better not push the wrong button with her. We became close like blood sisters. I began to tell her about the beatings, the cheating and the rapes. She became angry just from listening at my stories. One afternoon we had to work overtime and were scheduled to get off work at six o'clock p.m. By now I was riding with Earlene. I was so glad that "Tim" didn't have to take me to work anymore. We were sitting at our sewing machines chatting when all of a sudden "Tim" walks into the building with a very angry look on his face. I remember Earlene saying, "Don't be afraid Rosemary; he's not going to do anything to you! I got your back girl!" With the look Earlene gave him, he just looked at her and chuckled as he walked out of the factory. I dreaded going home that night. As usual, I was slapped when I walked in the door and was accused of things that I hadn't thought of doing. "This is it", I thought to myself.

As soon as Earlene picked me up for work the next morning, she saw the bruise on my face. She said, "Rosemary, I am not going to let you continue to go through this mess." We are going to wait until Friday evening and give him time to leave for the weekend. This was his weekly ritual. He would always leave on Friday evening and not return until Sunday night or either early Monday morning. Once "Tim" had left for the weekend, I immediately called Earlene to come and pick me up. Needless to say my nerves were frayed for fear of him coming back to the house. I took as much as I could and packed it in Earlene's car along with my baby girl and my son who was about 5 years old. My son (Donnie) always had an old soul. I remember how he would sit and talk to me and tell me everything would be alright. It used to break my heart when he would see "Tim" slapping me around the house. I remember one day when "Tim" was hitting me and Little Donnie (what we called him) boldly walked up to him and said he was going to call the police on him. How did my son even know about a police at such a young age? Anyway, as I was saying, I packed as much as I could in Earlene's car and me and my two children were finally leaving that place of horror. Earlene took us to her home and that is where we hid out for one week. I had to quit my job at Carolina

Casuals because I knew he would come there looking for me. Earlene lived down a dirt road and I really didn't like being there with two small children, but at least we were free from that horrible situation. Earlene had left a gun there with me and had told me not to be afraid to use it. I loved Earlene just like she was my sister and I really appreciated all that she had done for me, but I couldn't take living there anymore without a car, nothing to do and no one to talk to until she came home from work. Little did I know that God was still looking out for my children and I.

Remember my friend that I mentioned earlier that drove a green Laguna Super Sport? He was the one that fought for me when "Tim" had knocked me unconscious. I called him, not knowing if he would even answer the phone because I had broken up with him and went back to "Tim." Fortunately, he answered the phone and was willing to come and pick me up and take me back to my parent's house in Farmville, N.C. The same evening when I arrived back in Farmville, Earlene called me and said that "Tim" had found out where she lived and came to her house looking for me. I don't know to this day how he found out where I was. You see God was watching over me and my kids all the time. Earlene told me that she went to her door with her gun in her hand and told him to walk in her house if he dared to. Of course he left her house in a hurry.

## Chapter 5

Well, here I was back at my parent's house with two small children. I was so glad to be home again in my same old bed that I always slept in. My mom and dad eventually moved to a larger brick home near downtown Farmville and I and my kids moved with them. Soon after moving, I started working at another sewing plant called North State Garment Company. Lorraine was floor manager at North State also. I enjoyed working there, but it was nothing like the good times we had at USI Sewing Factory. Sometime I used to think that most of Farmville residents worked there (smiles). At this same house that was located on 910 South Main Street was where my dad became deathly ill from cirrhosis of the liver. He passed away at Wilson Memorial hospital that was located in Wilson, N.C. in the year of 1978. All I could think in my mind was that my mom was finally free. After so many years of abuse and neglect, she was finally free. Now she was able to go to church the way she always wanted to. Now she could sit on her front porch and face the traffic.

I eventually joined a mass choir that was directed by Mary Streeter. I need to mention also that the Streeter family was very close to us and saw many things that we endured. We had a ball traveling to different churches singing. But something was missing. I had not accepted Christ into my heart as my Lord and Savior. It was okay to travel and sing, but it was all in vain if I did not know the Lord. It was in that same choir that I met the man that I later married. After we were married, I gave my life to the Lord in June of 1977. That was the best decision I had ever made in my life! Through this marriage was born three beautiful children; two girls and one boy. The marriage lasted for thirteen years but ended in divorce. I now realize that in order to make it in a marriage, you must be equally yoked together and standing firm with one each other. It is a deadly thing to place other people in front of your wife or husband. And when you have part of the family constantly fighting you for no cause, it makes it even harder, especially when the spouse never defends you. We must know that there are always two sides to a story when you hear of the separation of two parties that are involved. It is so unfair to place all of the blame on one person. And it is sad when you have one party poisoning people behind your back and you are not there to defend yourself. I was always a quiet person and didn't speak up a lot for myself. I am what you call an introvert that keeps my feelings bottled up on the inside. Because of this unfortunate behavior that I adapted from my mom, I held a lot of things on the inside for years and would not share what actually happened in the marriage. Even to this day I have not shared some things that I really need to. To my readers, please whisper a prayer for me that God will totally heal me in every area.

Thanks so much! Soon after the break-up and after a year had passed, I married who I thought was the man of my dreams. I really believed that God was putting us together to have a powerful ministry He was very quiet and respectable towards me, and after he gave his life to Christ, we were married. I really cared a lot for him so please don't think that what I am sharing in my book is to destroy anybody's character. We became members at a small church in Snow Hill, N.C. and we enjoyed attending church there. It was at that same church that my husband, who I will call "Rick" (not his real name), received the baptism of the Holy Spirit. I knew in my heart that it was difficult for my children to accept "Rick" but I was praying constantly that they would eventually learn to love him. Unfortunately, one night after "Rick" and I returned home after attending church service, all of my children had left except my youngest son. On the coffee table was a small note that read, "Mom, it is time for us to leave." After reading the note, I collapsed on the floor and sobbed uncontrollably. I hardly got any sleep that night because I could not stop crying. Well, "I thought to myself," at least I still have my baby boy with me. At the time he was only 12 years old. But to my great disappointment, he also left me the next day. I pleaded with him to stay with me but he also said that he had to leave and live with his dad. I peeped out the window as I watched him walk around the corner to his oldest sister's house. I did not know that so much pain could reside in one small heart. After watching my baby boy disappear around the corner, I thought that this would surely be the end of me. I can only say that it was the grace and mercy of God that kept me from losing my mind or ending up in a mental institution. I was called derogatory names such as a whore or harlot. I was accused of child abandonment when I married "Rick," which was so far from my heart. As I before stated, it is never fair to hear a one-sided story when there are two parties involved. There is always more than what meets the eye. I hated myself for years for keeping my mouth shut. Who would ever believe me anyway? As the years began to pass, I always carried a deep emptiness in my soul because my children did not grow up with me. I managed to wear a smile and always used my comedic ways to keep myself aloof of what was taking place in my life. But on the inside of me I carried deep sadness, grief, and constant feelings of rejection. Because of intense slander and persecution from church folk, I stayed away from the church for many months. How can people that say they love the Lord try to destroy me like this? Will the pain ever go away? Will the tears ever stop? After being married to "Rick" for about a year, I began to notice abusive ways about him that I had never seen before. It first started with small disagreements that eventually escalated into bad arguments. There was one situation that happened before my kids moved out in which they heard us arguing in the bedroom. After arguing for a while, he decided to punch me in my stomach, which made me fall across my bed. I had already gone through so much already and now this. I tried to keep what I was going through from my children, but they always heard me sobbing through the thin walls of our apartment. This only made matters worse and made my kids hate him more along with all of the slander and hatred that was already being spread against me. Dear Lord, "I prayed," I thought I was honestly marrying someone that would love and treat me right. My kids left me, and now I am being abused again... After my children left, I could only ask within myself, "what next Lord?" Soon after, my dear mom passed away from kidney failure in May of 1993. Now the pain gets even deeper!! Lord can you please help me?! Can I make **it** without my mom? Whose shoulder can I lean on now with my mother gone? Why are all of these things happening at the same time? My mind felt as if it was going around in a whirlwind! And to top it all off, my mom's funeral was held on Mother's Day! What a day that I will never forget! "Rick" always had a problem with admiring other attractive women right in my presence. I am not a bad looking woman and I could never understand why he could never keep his eyes off other women, especially when you say you have accepted Christ into your life. It used to hurt so deeply, but like I shared earlier in my book, I always held my thoughts on the inside, which can be a very bad habit at times. I remember "Rick" and me taking Lorraine to the airport in Greenville, N.C. after our mom's funeral. At the time she was in the military and was stationed in Germany. To see her board that plane hurt me even greater, but I knew she had to go back to her job. After the hugs and tears and seeing her off, we headed back home. But before we could get out of the airport, a beautiful young lady walked in with her luggage. You would think "Rick" would have given me a little respect seeing we had just buried my mom on Mother's Day and had just seen my sister board that huge plane. To my disbelief, shock, and disappointment, "Rick" could not keep his eyes off of the young lady. I was quiet all the way back home, but as soon as we walked in the house, I could not hold my peace any longer. Why did you gaze at that woman like that, "I shouted?!" With a very cold reply he said, "If she was beautiful, she was just beautiful!" Never say that your mind will not snap when you are under a great deal of pressure because it certainly did happen to me. I remember my mind blanking out and I only saw black. The next thing I knew I had a knife in my hand and I was wielding it at him. Thankfully, he only sustained minor cuts. There I stood in my kitchen trembling and crying with the knife still in my hand. "Rick" left the house and stayed for a while. All I could do was sit on my couch and cry as I wondered what had I done to suffer like this.

Chapter 6

As time passed, I began to notice that "Rick" was experiencing rapid weight loss and having constant fevers. I suggested that he go to the doctor and see what was going on with his body. After several test and a biopsy, the doctor discovered that he had a lung disease known as Sarcoidosis. He informed me that the medication that he was prescribing for him would cause him to go through mood swings. I thought to myself could it get any worse. There were times that "Rick" coughed so violently (one of the effects of Sarcoidosis), that he would lose oxygen from his brain and faint. This is a condition known as syncope. I cannot count the times that he fainted and hit the floor very hard. He was too heavy for me to try and pick up, so I had to let him lie there until he regained consciousness. You would think that he would have been more appreciative of me by now, but I never really felt appreciated. The coughing seemed to lessen after a period of time, and I was very thankful for that. Eventually, I started working in the school system as a substitute school teacher and a teacher in the after-school program. I loved working at school with the children.. The students always showed me a great deal of love, and would applaud when I walked into the classroom. There was a time when my name was defamed at a particular school, and most of the students at the school went into the hallways and protested going back to class if certain people did not leave me alone. Wow! I didn't know that they loved me so much! This was a period in my life that feeling the love from the students was much needed, but I still could not stand the whispers and slander that was coming from "church folk." Not being able to deal with the persecution, rejection, and pain, "Rick" suggested that we move away to Smithfield, N.C. Feeling as though no one really cared if I lived or died, I complied with his wishes. Big mistake! Had I known what I was going to endure, I would have never left.

Living in a city where I knew no one was very difficult. I had to become accustomed to a new environment that I really did not like. Having previous experience in the school system, I decided to work in the public schools in Johnston County. This seemed to be my only outlet to find relief from the arguments that only grew worse. I remember one Sunday morning I decided to get dressed, not really knowing where I was going. All I know is that I needed to find a church to attend. While driving down Market Street in Smithfield, I noticed a lady that was beautifully dressed. At first glance I could tell that she was a Christian. I pulled over to where she was standing and told her that I was looking for a church to visit. She stated that it was God that led me to her because she was on the way to her church. After arriving, I found myself getting a little excited because I was finally able to attend someone's church. Anita (her real name), turned out to be a very good friend during the entire time that I lived in Smithfield. There were days and nights when I drove over to her house because "Rick" had knocked me on the floor or verbally abused me. I never knew that words could be so cutting and destructive to the human soul! I have always been a kind-hearted person, and could not understand why I was continually going through this cruel cycle of abuse in my life. I finally came to the realization that I was living under a generational curse that was passed down from my parents and their family. Four years had been enough for me! I wasn't making enough money in the school system to survive on my own, and I definitely did not want to continue to live there anyway. I reached out to the next to my oldest daughter (Tristaca) and asked her **if I** could please move in with her back in Greenville, N.C. By that time, my body was immersed with stress. I was having major panic attacks, heart spasms for three months straight, light-headedness, weight loss, insomnia, severe constipation, and nervousness, just to name a few side effects. Some I will not mention here in my book. Thankfully, my daughter lovingly took me in. I could only lie on her couch and drink ginger ale and eat crackers all day. Really didn't have much of an appetite. Those of you that are reading my book and have gone through any type of abuse, you know that the next thing an abuser does is promise you that they will change and treat you better. This is their way of getting you back into their clutches and control. After staying with my daughter for a little while, "Rick" continued to travel back and forth to Greenville asking me to come back. Unfortunately, I believed his lies and deceit and fell right back into the same cycle of abuse. It is so sad when people look at a couple and believe that they are happy and living a life of bliss. Most abusers are quiet or display the perfect attitude in the public's eye, which makes it difficult for the onlookers to see what is really taking place behind closed doors. What is called the "honey moon period" only lasted for about a month, and then the name calling, emotional and physical abuse started right back again. Here I was again having to constantly forgive and trying to make the marriage work. I really didn't want to go through persecution from the church anymore, so I tried my very best to stick it out (another poor choice on my part). We eventually moved back to Greenville and things got a little better for a while. In 2001, I felt compelled to start a women's ministry because of what I had endured in my life. Reconstructed Women's Fellowship Ministry, Inc. was established to help young girls and women who had sustained sexual and domestic violence. At first, the ministry seemed to be growing and doing pretty well, and I was very excited and thankful for the new women that I was meeting. Although my ministry was established to help other women, it was also a great help to me. I was finally seeing something positive in my life. Unfortunately, the symptoms of Sarcoidosis began to appear back in "Rick's" body and carne back with a vengeance. His breathing became worse and he was given oxygen that he had to use on a daily basis. Having to take care of him and take him to constant doctor's appointments, I decided to put my women's ministry on hold. The violent coughing and fainting spells started again, and he was also very difficult to get along with. Many times I questioned God and asked Him what I had done to deserve all of this. During the time of "Rick's illness, my sister Lorraine became very ill. I remember praying with her over the phone for 40 days. By faith, I spoke healing over her body for those 40 days. I promised her that God would heal her and that she was not going to die anytime soon. Lorraine had already gone through so much already with the murder of her son by his wife. (RIP Bill). Through all of this, I continued to be strong for her and speak faith and healing over her body. Although I could not understand at first, I had to accept that God had another plan. She passed away in November of 2004 after battling cancer. I thought I was really going to lose my mind, but through a special word on television that God spoke to me through Prophetess Juanita Bynum, I was able to move on. I still miss my sister every day. She was my buddy, she was my friend.

## Chapter 7

As the months and years went by "Rick's" condition only grew worse. There were several trips back and forth to the hospital and also to Chapel Hill, N.C. where he stayed for a week. My youngest son (Willie) had joined the USAF and was stationed in Germany. He had heard what I was going through and that "Rick" had been sent to Chapel Hill for further treatment. Through the aid of the Red Cross and his job, he was allowed to come home and stay with me for a week. He will never know how much I needed him with me and how much strength he was to me. I will never forget the breakfast that he cooked for me every morning and brought the plate to my bed and said, "It's time to get up Ma." Boy, did I hate to see that week come to an end! Getting up on that Friday morning and watching my son pack his bags was a bit overwhelming for me. Before I took him to the airport, he wanted to take me to Denny's restaurant to have breakfast. I was doing all I could not to break down and cry in front of him. My baby boy has always been a very comedic person ever since he was a little child, so of course he was saying things to make me laugh. Well, the time had come for me to take him to the airport. I honestly felt like a thrown away old dish rag. We stood and talked for a few minutes until we saw the huge plane come down that long run-way. If only he knew the pain and sadness I was feeling on the inside. After giving me a big hug and telling me he loved me, he turned and walked away. After boarding the airplane, he looked out the plane's window and waved at me and then disappeared out of sight. Without being able to control myself, I collapsed against the large window that I was looking through and began to cry out loud. I still do not know until this day where this kind-hearted lady came from. She was very soft-spoken and said to me, "That must be your baby boy." How did she know that and where did she come from? Her kind words only made me cry even harder. She gently rubbed my back and told me that God would take care of my son and everything was going to be alright. Was she an angel? I guess I'll never know. After arriving back home and still feeling heart-broken and alone, I held on to what the nice lady had told me at the airport. Later on that day I received a call from Chapel Hill that "Rick" was being transported by ambulance back to our home around 10:00 p.m. that night. The doctor's had given him the grim news that his lungs were beyond repair and that he was too sick to receive a lung transplant. I never knew any of this until "Rick" passed away. The last few months of his life were very difficult. He was placed on oxygen again 24-7 because it was very difficult for him to breathe. I had to bathe him because he was unable to do for himself anymore. Well, it was time for me to take him to his next doctor's appointment. He was moving really slow on that morning and had to sit down several times before I could get him to the truck. Once he got inside the truck, he started experiencing another violent coughing episode. As he continued to cough, he began spitting up blood. It frightened me and I ran to get the phone to call the rescue squad. He begged me not to call them, but there was nothing else I could do. After arriving at the hospital and taken into the emergency room, "Rick" could not breathe at all. There I stood crying as I watched him lose all of his breath. He managed to say to me that everything was going to be alright Rose. Those were the last words that he ever said to me. I felt myself going to the floor but a doctor ran over and caught me and took me out of the room. When the doctor came back to get me, I was not prepared for what I saw. There he lay with a large tube down his throat with his eyes wide open as they rolled back and forth. I couldn't stand seeing Him that way, so I turned and ran back out of the room. There I was in that small waiting room crying again and feeling like I was about to lose my mind once more. That was on a Wednesday and on that Friday morning he was gone. I never saw him again because I was not able to see him lying in a coffin. "Rick" passed away in March of 2007.

The days that lie ahead of me were very difficult. Although "Rick" didn't treat me well at times, I cared a lot for him. The grief was unbearable, so I decided to attend grief counseling classes, which were a great help to me. There I met other people that were going through the grief process as well. It really makes you feel better when you can share your story and listen to other people's story. After making it through those first difficult months, I began working at the Job Link Career Center in Greenville, N.C. I loved working there because I met new people every day. I had my own office and began to feel like somebody again in my life. I was finally feeling at peace again and was experiencing a new joy in my life. What would I have done without Christ in my life? I would have never made it without His help and guidance. Because of the love of God in my heart, I was able also to forgive my dad and all others that had caused me harm. I eventually met someone else and we were later married. I began to work more diligently with my women's ministry, which helped me also to build my self-esteem. A few years later, I was blessed to graduate with honors at Liberty University's campus in Lynchburg, Virginia. On May 10, 2015, I received an Associate of Arts in religion. Such a great accomplishment in my life gave me an awesome feeling of being special. I can only say, "To God be all of the glory!" This is not the end of my story, but I am going to stop for now. Please stay tuned for the next chapter of my life. I pray that as you took a journey with me through my life, that you were blessed and inspired by my true life story. Maybe you cried a little, and maybe you rejoiced in knowing that God kept me through all of my life's trials. Thank you to all of my readers that took the time to read my book. Through it all, God has been my strength and my peace. There is a famous cliche that says, "I don't look like what I have been through!"

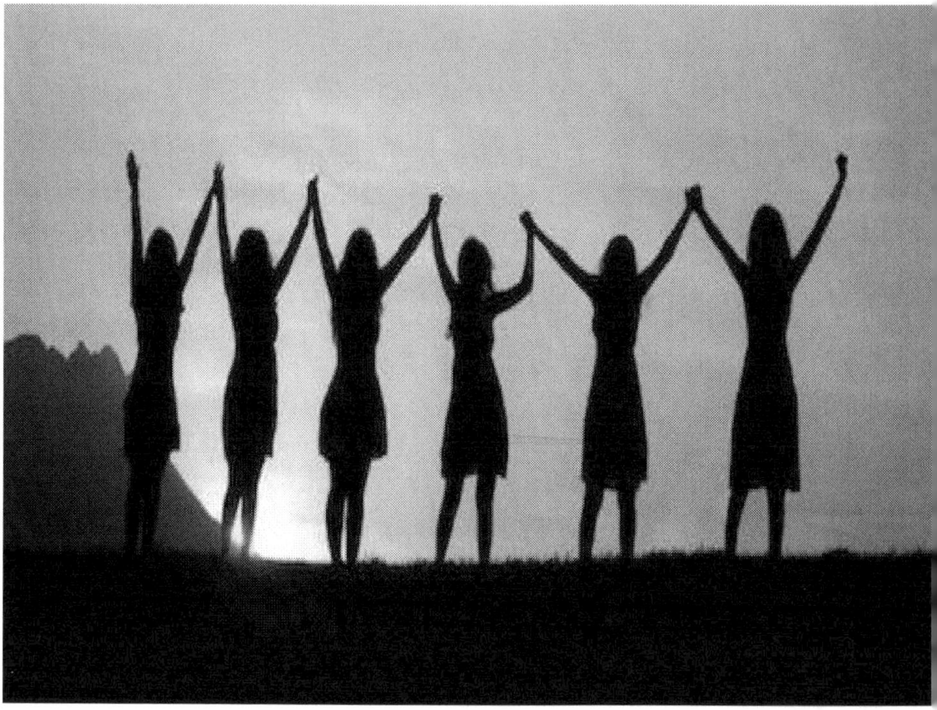

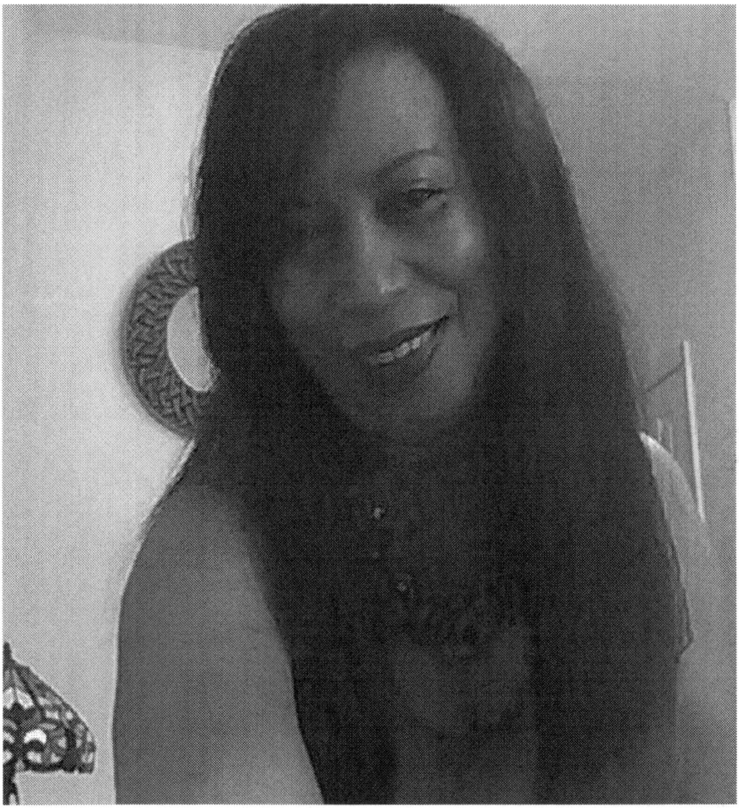

Made in the USA
Columbia, SC
21 June 2017